BROKEN STARS

GAZA POEMS

Buff Whitman-Bradley

ISBN: 978-1-967022-18-2

Fomite
Burlingon, VT
fomitepress.com

For David Glick 1944-2025
He never gave up.

The genocide and ethnic cleansing in Gaza continue. We have been unable to stop it. We cry out. We line the streets. We visit our congressional representatives, We occupy. We break the rules. We are punished for demanding an end to the horror. Horror is the way nation states operate. Israel is no greater criminal than every other colonialist country, every other barbaric, amoral murdering, destroying, brutalizing nation that ever was. Massacre and slaughter, carnage and devastation and annihilation are how the US and its little brother Israel do business.

The darkness around us is deep.
-William Stafford

We write our names with crimson mist!
We end the hymn with our flesh.
Here we will die. Here, in the final passage.
Here or there, our blood will plant olive trees.
-Mahmoud Darwish

I could not help but think

As we stood out in the first rain
Of the season
Watching our granddaughters play soccer
I could not help but think
Of the children of Gaza
Who must be profoundly traumatized
By the bombs that are falling like rain
All around them,
Who must be frightened beyond anything
Our little granddaughters can imagine,
Who must be wondering
What it is like to die.

As we stood out in the first rain
Of the season
Watching our granddaughters
Get soaked by the downpour,
Get wonderfully, joyfully muddy
And happily exhausted,
Mom and Dad, Grandma and Grandpa
Cheering them on,
I could not help but think
Of the crushed and mangled and charred bodies
Of the children of Gaza
Pulled from great smoking mounds
Of bombed hospitals and schools
And community centers and apartment buildings
As their bewildered spirits
Stumbled through the wreckage
Wondering what they had done
In their brief lives
To be treated with such brutality.

As we stood out in the first rain
Of the season

Watching the game come to an end,
The girls giving high-fives
To their opponents,
The coaches presenting each player
With a trophy,
The parents loading up the cars
To head home for snacks,
A change of clothes,
Maybe warm baths,
I could not help but think
Of the children of Gaza . . .

Gaza haikus

--Palestinian parents in Gaza are writing their children's names on their small bodies so they can be identified when pulled from the rubble.

Mama, I'm afraid
The bombs are looking for me
They will explode me

Don't cry little one
I'll write your name on your arm
To keep you alive

Is it magic, Mama?
Is there magic in my name
To keep me alive?

Yes my little one
Your name is filled with love
So you will be safe

Write my name, Mama
Write it on my arms and legs
Write it on my heart

Yes, my little one
I'll write your name everywhere
All over the earth

I'm sleepy, Mama
Will you sleep here next to me
And tell me stories

Yes, my little one
Stories about how great love
Keeps children alive

I hope that great love
Will protect me from the bombs
I love you, Mama

Sleep now, little one
I will be here all night long
Saying your sweet name

Deep in the rubble

Deep in the rubble
Where slivers of light
Sneak their way past
Huge blocks of blasted concrete
To briefly flash on the retinas
Of the little children trapped there,
Where sounds become impossibly faint
And contort themselves into
Alien noises
As they grope their way
Through the remains of collapsed hospitals
Shattered apartment buildings
Demolished schools
On their way to the eardrums
Of the little children trapped there,
The little children trapped there
Are exhausted from weeping,
Exhausted from desperately calling out
For mama and papa,
Exhausted from the horror
Of being unable to move
And alone in the dark,
Exhausted from wondering,
"What did I do wrong? What did I do wrong?
What did I do wrong?"

Deep in the rubble
The little children trapped there
Still have hope
That they will be rescued
And returned to their parents' arms,
To their homes and families and friends.
Deep in the rubble
The little children trapped there
Are falling asleep in spite of the pain,

In spite of the fear,
In spite of the terrifying whine
Of killer jets overhead
And the earth-shaking thunder of monster bombs
Pulverizing the city.
Falling asleep
The little children trapped there
Quietly tell themselves
That mama and papa will find them soon,
Quietly tell themselves
That everything will be all right.

When the children return from the dead

When the children return from the dead
Still wrapped in their ragged, bloody shrouds
Still gaunt from starvation
Still filled with shrapnel
Still armless and legless
Still perforated with bullet holes . . .
When the children return from the dead
Still carrying the ragged stuffed animals
And the tattered blankets
That comforted them during the bombings
During the days trapped under rubble
During the artillery shelling
During the sniping
During the drone attacks
And the missiles fired by jet fighters
And the helicopters strafing . . .
When the children return from the dead
To look for their parents
Their siblings
Their grandparents and uncles and aunts and
cousins
To learn what has become of them
To learn if they are still alive
To learn if their house is still standing
If their bicycles and soccer balls and games and
toys
Are still where they left them . . .
When the children return from the dead
They will be as innocent as they always were
But now more wise than the greatest
philosophers
More compassionate than the holiest saints
More generous in spirit than the most righteous
among us
And in their innocence and wisdom

Their compassion and generosity
The children will ask us why they were
murdered
Why we allowed the killing to take place
But the children will not wait for our answer
They will leave the question
To remain lodged inside us
Like a ball of rusted barbed wire
Or shards of broken glass
And then the children will return
To be forever among the dead

The children of the dead

The children of the dead
Wander through the blasted landscape
Pulling little wagons
Piled high with broken toys,
Ripped and eyeless stuffed animals,
Empty bowls
And the enormous absences
Created by 2000-lb. bombs
And spectral drones.

The faces of the children of the dead
Are smeared with dirt and blood and tears
They have no shoes
They wear torn t-shirts
With pictures of American celebrities
Emblazoned on them
They wear baseball caps
Of the Yankees, the Dodgers, the Giants, the
Cubs
They wear the apparel of American capital
American hegemony
The apparel of USA & Co.
As they stumble along the rubbled roads
Not knowing where they are going
Or what they are looking for
Or how they will die.

I would like to tell the children of the dead:
Tomorrow stones will be flowers
Bombs will fall upwards
And melt in the sun
Machine guns will choke on their own vomit
The vicious killers rampaging
Through your streets
And through your dreams

Will evaporate into puffs of fetid breath
To be swept away
By lilac-scented winds.
I would like to tell the children of the dead:
You are the heroes of this story
Not the villains
You are the seeds that will sprout
All over the ruined earth
You will make olive trees grow
You will make Palestine bloom.

Broken stars

We do not know
How to think about
The genocide in Gaza.
We do not have a way
To understand the broken stars
In Gaza's sky.
We do not know
How to make sense
Of the bloody sands
On Gaza shores.
With utter disbelief
And nausea
We listen to reports
Of rescue workers
Gathering pieces of dead children.
We watch videos
Of Israeli soldiers
Celebrating their torture
And rape
Of Palestinian men and women
And are heartbroken
That human decency can be
So lightly set aside.
We look at photographs
Of the boneyard called Gaza
Wondering how many bodies
Lie silently howling
Beneath its 140 square miles
Of rubble and ruin.
Our minds' eyes cannot unsee the blood
On the sands of Gaza's shores.
Our hearts convulse in grief
For Gaza's shattered stars.

Vocabularies of outrage

Children are dying in Gaza
Faster than we can find words
To describe the horror.
Whole families in Gaza
Are being annihilated at such a rapid rate
That our vocabularies of outrage
Cannot keep up.
How many times can we say *slaughter*
Without losing the ability
To feel its impact?
How often can we pronounce *genocide*
And not grow numb
To what it is saying to us?
Do we need new words, urgent words, ferocious
words
To convey the profound evil
That is occurring in Gaza?
Do we need dangerous words,
Deadly words, murderous words?
Words that fire bullets?
Words that explode?
Words that bury children beneath rubble?
Words that sever limbs,
That rip out intestines,
That decapitate?
Language cannot keep up
With the relentless cruelty,
The ceaseless barbarity,
That powerful nations
Are enacting upon the bodies of the innocent.
Words become ghosts
In the houses of the dead.

Those who have survived

When did they teach us
How to grieve?
I do not remember.
When did they teach us
How to live with a bottomless,
Emptiness-infested abyss
Deep inside us?
I do not recall.
A loved one leaves us
And we are left to fend for ourselves,
To walk on only one leg,
To gaze at the world
Through a single eye,
To trudge and slog all on our own
Across trackless immensities,
Vast tundras and deserts of absence,
To awaken every day
Unable to escape the leaden dreams
That sink us in despair?
Did someone explain grief to us?
Did someone explain the mute howl
Echoing down the long corridors
Of our blood?
Was there a wise old friend
Who led us into the forest
To listen for guidance
In the conversations of owls?
Was there a boon companion
Whose loving silence
Inhabited our body,
Balm to the jagged lacerations of our soul,
Comfort to our blindly bewildered heart?
Who mentored us in the art of loss?
When did they teach us
How to grieve?

High up in October oaks

Sitting in the living room
On a warm autumn night
With the front door open
To the evening air,
We talk about family matters,
How the grandchildren
Are faring in school,
What our kids will be doing
For the holidays.
We hear the owls conversing also,
And a car drive by once in a while,
And a neighbor calling for her kids
To come home.
And into the midst of that calmness
And quietness
There comes a sudden explosion,
Then another,
And another,
Sirens blaring,
Buildings blown to pieces,
People screaming, howling, wailing,
Running out of collapsing apartments and
hospitals,
Parents and children
Crying out for each other,
The horribly injured pleading for help,
Ones crushed beneath debris
Moaning their last words.
On a warm autumn night
In Sebastopol, California,
We are hearing the sounds
Of an ongoing genocide
Happening 7000 miles away
In Gaza and Lebanon,
Being perpetrated

By the war criminal state of Israel.
We are hearing the dying
Plead for help,
Plead for someone
To make the explosions stop,
Lying armless or legless in the ashes and dust,
Begging for Mama or Papa,
Husband or wife,
To come and embrace them,
To shield them,
To save them.
They lie in thickening pools
Of their own blood and tears
As the massacre continues,
As Israeli soldiers
Envelop themselves in carnage,
Wrap themselves in slaughter,
Don the undergarments
Of women they have raped and murdered,
Smear their uniforms with gore.
And as a little child soon to be no more
Whimpers in the rubble,
The owls outside our house,
On a warm night at the beginning of autumn,
Whisper about bottomless grief and sorrow
From high up
In the October oaks.

Invasive species

Was this what the world
Was meant to be,
This screeching, brawling,
Murderous conglomeration
Of vicious, self-aggrandizing
Psychopathic, homicidal
Brutes and barbarians
Who fabricate preposterous
Utterly nonsensical excuses
For their unspeakable cruelties?

What sort of creatures are these
Who gleefully pump bullets
Into the brains of infants and toddlers?
Who happily dismember and decapitate,
Crush and incinerate
Children attempting to escape
Their bombs?
What kind of ghouls take delight
In mercilessly raping prisoners,
In eviscerating pregnant women?

Was all of this encoded
In the DNA of Homo sapiens?
Is the mangling of the soul
And the murdering of each other
Our genetic destiny?
Or is there living among us
An invasive species,
Like cane toads
And mountain pine beetles
And feral pigs,
That wreak havoc in the natural world?
What can we do about these moral mutants
Who have so disfigured and contorted our world

And brought the human project
To the brink
Of utter annihilation?

Israeli sniper
--Physicians in Gaza report large numbers of dead
children with a single wound in the head or chest.

The sniper sits in a third-story window
Scanning the rubble
For any signs of life.
He is growing bored.
He wishes to do the work
That he is best at.
He presses his eye
Up against the lens of the scope
Perched atop his high-powered rifle.
He loves his weapon,
How exquisitely it is crafted,
The weight substantial enough
For him to steady it easily
But not so heavy
That instantaneous adjustments of aim
Are cumbersome and clumsy.
The sniper is thinking of his family,
His wife and two little daughters,
Wondering what they are doing today,
Wondering if the girls miss their daddy.
He feels in his shirt pocket
For the small silver picture frame
He took from a destroyed house yesterday.
It will make a nice gift for his wife..
He hopes he can also find souvenirs
For each of the girls,
A couple of dolls, maybe
Or some stuffed animals.
They are always so excited
When he brings them something home from
work.
Suddenly he notices movement
Over there near the kitchen without walls,

Behind the refrigerator.
He stops thinking and watches
With brutal, single-minded focus.
Yes.
Someone is there.
Don't be impatient.
Wait for a clear shot.
A small child covered in dust
Wanders out into the open
Looking dazed and disoriented.
He cannot tell if it is a girl or a boy.
The child seems to be crying
But it is difficult from up here
To see if the streaks on its face
Are mud or blood or tears.
Probably all three.
The sniper chuckles to himself.
This is an easy one, he thinks,
As he squeezes the trigger.

IDF sniper school school

You will hunt yourself down
Over and over again.
You will sit alone
In an upper-story room
Of a bombed-out building,
Your IWI DAN .338 pressed against your shoul-
der
As you scan the rubble
Of the blasted landscape
With the attached state-of-the art scope
Until you see yourself crawling out
Into the open
From behind a burned-out automobile.
You will place that image of you
Dragging yourself through the dust
Into the exact center
Of the scope's cross hairs
And gently squeeze the trigger.
You will blow your own brains out
With a single shot,
After which you will report your success
To headquarters
Using your cell phone,
And broadcast the video you took of the kill
On social media.
Then you will sit quietly once more
By the window of the room
In the ruined building
Scanning the debris
For your next kill.
And whether it is a weeping old woman,
A teenager in charred rags,
A bloody and bewildered toddler,
It will always be you.

Little brown birds

When the slaughtered children of Gaza
Leave their mangled, crushed,
Shredded, dismembered bodies
They become little brown birds
That flit and fly all about
Among the ruins
That were once their homes
And their schools and neighborhoods.

When the massacred children of Gaza
Fly above the snipers
Whose bullets punctured their hearts
And shattered their skulls
They chirp their songs
Of carnage and slaughter
But the snipers claim
That they cannot hear them.

When the murdered children of Gaza
Perch on debris near a tank
That repeatedly ran over them
Until their bodies were little more
Than puddles of gore
They sing of mechanized murder
Of flesh pulverized and liquified
But the tank crew claim
That they cannot hear them.

When the annihilated children of Gaza
Come upon squads of infantry
Who used them as human shields
Who tortured them and mocked them
Who took their toys as souvenirs
To give to their own children
They chirrup sad melodies

About the death of the soul
But the soldiers claim
That they cannot hear them.

The snipers, the tank crew, the ground troops
Do hear the little brown birds
The singing pierces them to their core
Where their humanity once resided
But which is now inhabited by nothing
Except the heartbreak and horror
Of the songs of the little brown birds.

After a good long rest

After a good long rest
During which he had time
To renew and rejuvenate
His wounded body
His wounded pride
His wounded plans
And the lies he tells himself
The monster is stirring again
And showing signs
Of wishing to resume
His slaughter of innocents
His massacre of children
His rape and murder of women.

After a good long rest
The reinvigorated monster
Is energetically justifying
To himself and the world
His heinous crimes against humanity
By claiming to be victim
Rather than perpetrator,
By claiming to be righteous
Rather than evil,
By claiming to be chosen
Rather than damned.

After a good long rest
The serial war criminal
Gets back to work
Taking inventory
Of the tools of genocide
Provided by his good friend
Mr. USA, INC.
Who is delighted that his vicious little ally
Is itching to return to the fray

And butcher away.

After a good long rest
The bloodshot monster
Once again prevents food and water
From reaching his victims,
Once again prevents medicines
From reaching his victims,
Once again prevents doctors
From treating his victims,
Once again prevents the people of Palestine
From living safely
In their own land,
Once again polishes up his plans
For ethnic cleansing.

After a good long rest
The monster
Is combing through the rubble
Trying to find where
He might have lost his soul
During all of the hubbub and confusion
Of mass murder,
But all he can find
Are broken bodies
And the shattered pieces
Of who he thought he was.

The gates of hell

They have once more
Opened the gates of hell
To unleash their demonic rage
Upon the people who have the audacity
To wish for a life
In the land they have inhabited
For hundreds of years.

They have once more
Opened the gates of hell
To release the monstrous emissaries
Of duplicity and slaughter
Whose diplomatic vocabularies
Contain no words
For truth, for honor, for justice, for decency.

They have once more
Opened the gates of hell
To send forth young men and women
With their titanium spines,
Their metallic grins,
Their white phosphorous nightmares,
As satanic avengers against those
Who dare to dream
Of residing peacefully among the olive trees
Of their ancestors.

They have once more
Opened the gates of hell
In their own minds,
In their own hearts,
In their own lives,
And will come to realize
That those gates once opened
Do not close.

Utterly void

In order to commit
The heinous crimes
Their genocidal nation requires of them,
Soldiers must first submit
To a type of radical surgery
That removes
All the neural networks within them
That would cause them to feel
Compassion and empathy,
To feel shame and self-loathing,
To feel horror and disgust,
Radical surgery that empties them
Of humanity.

In order for settlers
To violently evict
Those whose families
Have lived in their homes
For generations,
To uproot and burn the orchards
That have sustained families
For centuries,
To raze villages
And remove them from maps,
First those settlers must be hollowed out,
Purged of all human decency,
Drained of the ability
To act unselfishly..

In order to enact genocide,
First a nation must
Murder its inner life
And bury its corpse,
Must purge all remnants,
However infinitesimal,

Of any sense that all others
Have value,
That all others deserve to live.
And in the depths
Of its demonic darkness
The nation must convince itself
That it is the light of the world.

And when a genocidal nation
Has vomited out its guts
So completely,
When its innards are thoroughly scoured
And utterly void,
There is nothing
It will not do.

Gaza: 7 short poems

Our imaginations no longer function
The gears clogged
By great heaps of amputated limbs.

***

Visiting doctors cannot believe the savagery.
Gutted children
Assure them it is true.

***

"Destroy all hospitals, destroy all schools,
Destroy all neighborhoods, destroy all life"
Chant the hollow ones.

***

There is a hole in the world
Through which can be heard
The approach of howling hordes.

***

We would like to think
That people collapse like bombed buildings
When their souls get up and leave.
But they continue to stand upright
Their steel eyes never blinking
Smug grins welded to their jaws.

***

Picture a beach, and children flying kites.
Picture killer drones.
Picture small corpses and red sand.

***

Words inscribed
On every speck of Gaza dust:
"Remember us."

Can you think of a name?

Can you think of a name
For those who murder masses
Without a whisper of regret?

Can you think of a name
For those who explode hospitals
With never a second thought?

Can you think of a name
For the rapists and torturers
Of prisoners?

Can you think of a name
For those who aim their shots
At the heads and hearts of children?

Can you think of a name
For those who withhold food
To starve thousands to death?

Can you think of a name
For those who eagerly provide the munitions
To commit genocide?

Can you think of a name
For those who argue
That the fault lies with the victims?

Is it *monster?* Is it *demon?*
Is it *ghoul* or *fiend* or *abomination?*
Is it *ogre* or *cannibal* or *the living dead?*

Is it burning coals on the tongue?
Is it broken glass in the throat?
Is it serpents in the gut?

Can you think of a name
For those who watch whole families get slaugh-
tered
But are unable to stop it?

Can you think of a name for bottomless sorrow
and grief?

Photo of a Gaza child

In the photo from Gaza
A small child
Is standing in a line
That may or may not
Lead to food.
The child is not wearing a shirt,
His ribs look almost as if
They are on the outside of his body
Rather than inside him.

I have been hungry.
You have been hungry.
We've gone home
To grab a sandwich
Or stopped for a burger
At a fast-food joint.
The look on the little boy's face
Speaks of a hunger so enormous,
So profound and devastating,
You and I cannot fully grasp
What he is experiencing.

The little boy is probably going to die.
Something in him
Has been desperately fighting
Against his likely death,
But he is weakening.
He has had no food
For more days than he can count.
His little body is giving out,
Not surrendering,
But increasingly unable
To continue the struggle
No matter how much
He wants to live.

This beautiful little Palestinian boy,
All children of Gaza,
All Palestinians living in that nightmare,
Are being systematically starved
By those who have lost the right
To call themselves human beings
As their own version
Of a "final solution"
Plays out in Gaza,
As they lay plans
To ethnically cleanse an entire populace
And turn their homeland
Into real estate
For the true believers.

The little boy is still standing in line,
Holding a cracked bowl
In both hands
Extending it to the world
And asking the world
To make this stop.

**Congress Urged to Act Now
As Israel Moves to 'Occupy and
Flatten' Gaza and Starvation Worsens**
--headline on Common Dreams, 5/16/25

Like an enormous and ignorant beast
Congress listens to tales
Of genocide
With its mouth hanging open,
Slobber dripping down its chin,
A baffled look on its flaccid face,
Poised dumbly atop a heap of rancid legislation,
Waiting to be fed.

In Gaza, with a vast arsenal
Congress has provided,
The Israeli Defense Forces
Continue to lay waste to the wasted land,
Attempting to erase all traces
Of their Original Sin.
Good people everywhere
Condemn the Israeli crime of crimes
And decry the enabling Congress,
Which replies to all criticism with a thundering
"Huh?"

In addition to its cerebral deficit,
Congress suffers from a shrunken and deflated
heart,
For it is unable to empathize
With the victims of its weaponry piñata,
Unable to muster up one iota of compassion
For the families decimated,
The children amputated,
The parents decapitated,
The doctors and journalists and ambulance
drivers

And teachers and taxi drivers and shop keepers
Erased.

Empathy requires imagination,
Imagination requires intelligence,
Intelligence requires courage,
Congress requires donations
For services rendered.

Blasted Acres
--reports have surfaced of a Trump administra-
tion plan to move a million Gazans to Libya

Wasteland Real Estate Associates
Is proud to announce
The opening of a new development
In North Africa.
Blasted Acres,
In the Mediterranean nation of Libya,
Is now ready
For the resettlement of Palestinian refugees
Who have been ethnically cleansed
From their homeland.

Blasted Acres offers an environment
That will make the refugees feel
Right at home.
Years of civil war,
Initiated by the wholesale destruction of Libya
By the euphemistically-named
NATO forces
Has created a lunar landscape
Almost entirely devoid of the resources
Necessary to support
A decent existence,
But ideal for pitching the tents
Whole families of refugees
Have inhabited in Gaza
Since their homes and communities
Were bombed into nonexistence.

Having been forcibly removed
From their decimated homeland,
Refugees will be welcomed
To their Libyan tent cities
By various armed militias

Eager to recruit them.
Just like home,
The refugees will not be able
To find work
And will be forced to rely
On meager resources
From international aid agencies.
Just like home
Their tents will not protect them
From extreme weather.
And just as they were treated
Like intruders in their homeland
So too will they be treated like intruders
In the ruined land of Libya.

As the genocide in Palestine continues,
Israelis are reassured to know
That they will not have to carry out
The grueling and messy work
Of total extermination,
That they can count on
The massive resources of their US collaborators
To transport all the Palestinians
Who remain alive in Gaza
To their new home
In Libya's Blasted Acres.

You promised
--a picture posted on Common Dreams,
5/22/25

The little Palestinian child
Is almost not there,
So absent is flesh
From his skeleton.
In the photo we see him
Lying on a table
Looking directly at the camera
With enormous brown eyes.
He has his tiny hand
Wrapped around the thumb
Of an adult
Who is mostly
Out of the picture.
Beneath him is a fleece blanket
On which there are pictured
Pink and blue squares,
A white star inside a blue cloud,
A tan teddy bear.
Perhaps it is the blanket
He has slept with every night
Since he was born,
A blanket that comforts him,
That makes him feel safe.
And as this little wasting-away baby,
This starving infant,
Looks deep into the lens
At you and at me,
He has an enormous smile
On his face,
A baby's smile,
Completely open and loving,
Completely trusting,
Saying to us

"I know you will take care of me.
You promised."

Poll: 82% of Israelis want to expel Palestinians from Gaza; 47% want to kill every man, woman, child
—headline in Geopolitical Economy, June 30, 2025

In the books and stories I read
When I was a young boy
I learned how cruel
People could be to each other –
Torture chambers
In medieval castles,
Live human sacrifices
Atop Aztec pyramids,
Beheadings of political opponents,
Immolations and lynchings
Of the those
With the wrong skin color,
Or the wrong beliefs.
And as I read
I remember feeling so grateful
For human progress,
So grateful
To live in a time
When we no longer enacted such cruelties
On each other.

From books and stories I read
When I was somewhat older
I learned about World War II
And the atrocities perpetrated
In Dachau and Auschwitz
And Bergen-Belsen
And other murder factories.
I learned about the ongoing genocide
Of Native Peoples of the Americas.
I learned about European slaughters-for-profits

In Asia and Africa,
And in the daily news,
I learned of mass murders
In Viet Nam and Yugslavia and Iraq,
To name but a few.

I am an old man now
Watching every day as Israel
Commits unspeakable atrocities
Against the people of Palestine,
Murdering whole families,
Incinerating little children,
And proclaiming the virtue
Of such wickedness.

When I was a young boy
I believed that I lived in a world
That had outgrown
The horrific, psychotic madness
Of the torture and slaughter
And ethnic cleansing
Of our fellow beings,
But the thug state of Israel
And its bevy of eager enablers
Have shown me
That I was wrong.

Over 5,000 Gaza Children Treated for Malnutrition in May Alone
--headline on Common Dreams, 6/19/25

The pictures are heartbreaking.
Infants and toddlers
Grown impossibly thin,
Wispy almost,
As if they were blades of grass
Tied together to make dolls.
The expressions on their faces
Are utterly innocent.
They are not crying.
Their enormous eyes
Are looking directly at us.
They are calm,
They do not weep,
Do not sob,
But quietly plead,
Telling us that they don't know
Why they are suffering,
Telling us they don't know
How to help themselves,
And asking us if we would please
Do something to make it better.
"Please," they soundlessly implore,
"Please take care of us."

What kind of nightmare world
Are we living in,
Where starving children intentionally
Is used as a weapon?
What kind of ugly existence is this
That is dominated
By the most grotesque of thugs
Accumulating great wealth and power
No matter the cost

In order to accumulate
More wealth and power?
How do we look into
The deep and baffled eyes
Of a dying child
And explain that
To the "leaders of the free world"
Her life does not matter?

The reddening dust

A father is walking in a large crowd
With his two little boys,
Holding each one by a hand.
They are on their way
To get food for their family
From the distribution point
Identified by Israel.
Like all little boys,
His toddler sons
Want to play with other children
They meet on their way.
But their father tells them
They must not dawdle,
They must not run about
Amongst all the other walkers,
They must not go where their father
Cannot see them.

Still, the boys act silly,
Teasing each other,
Throwing handfuls of dirt
Up into the air,
Singing nonsensical songs.

All at once
The air screams,
The people in the crowd panic
And begin running blindly
In every direction.
The boys grip their father's hands
As tightly as they can.
There is an enormous explosion
That shakes the ground
And then all is silent.

Still holding their father's large hands,
The two little boys lie on the ground,
No longer hungry,
Not wanting to run and play anymore,
Not wanting to make jokes
Or trick their friends.
Their father lies between them,
Unmoving in the reddening dust,
Not far from the distribution point
Identified by Israel.

ACKNOWLEDGMENTS

All of the poems in this book were originally published in *Dissident Voice*. I am grateful to the editors for seeing some worth in them.

About the Author

Buff Whitman-Bradley's poems have appeared in many print and online journals. He is the author of six books of poetry and three nonfiction books. He podcasts his poetry at thirdactpoems.podbean.com and lives in northern California with his wife, Cynthia.

Books by Buff Whitman-Bradley

Poetry
b. eagle, poet
The Honey Philosophies
At the Driveway Guitar Sale
The heron could be lost
And What Will We Sing?
A Friendly Little Tavern Somewhere Near the Pleiades

Nonfiction
Endings: A Book About Death
Where Do I Belong? A Kids' Guide to Step-Families
Growing from Wordplay Into Poetry
About Face: Military Resisters Turn Against War (ed., with Sara Lazare & Cynthia Whitman-Bradley

www.ingramcontent.com/pod-product-compliance
Lightning Source LLC
Chambersburg PA
CBHW031238120626
46545CB00003B/1177